THE MASS:

ITS MYSTERIES REVEALED

GEORGE P. MORSE

CATHOLICS COMMITTED TO SUPPORT THE POPE

Nihil Obstat: William E. May, Ph.D.
                  Censor Deputatus

Imprimatur: Most Reverend William E. Lori
                  Vicar General for the
                  Archdiocese of Washington

                  August 21, 1998
                  Feast of Pope St. Pius X

The Nihil Obstat and Imprimatur are official declarations that a book or pamphlet is free of doctrinal or moral error. No implication is contained therein that those who have granted the Nihil Obstat and Imprimatur agree with the contents, opinions or statements expressed.

CNS photo by Arturo Mari

Copyright © 1999

ISBN No. 0-9672595-0-9

George P. Morse

DEDICATION AND ACKNOWLEDGMENT

This booklet is prayerfully dedicated to our children and grandchildren – and to all children and grandchildren – begging our Divine Savior and Redeemer to grant to each one the opportunity and the commitment to search and find the limitless treasures waiting for them in a deep love for the Mass.

It is especially dedicated with love and admiration for Rev. Robert F. Morse, M.M., who lived just ten days after his ordination, but long enough to receive the priceless gift of being able to "offer Christ to God" one time, in his single Mass.

With gratitude, we offer thanks to those who helped make possible this booklet –

My esteemed colleague of many years in the publishing of our eleven volume series of PRECIS OF OFFICIAL CATHOLIC TEACHING, an eminent theologian and great friend, Rev. Msgr. Peter J. Elliott, without whose patient guidance at every step along the way this booklet would not have been written. Msgr. Elliott, now Episcopal Vicar for the Archdiocese of Melbourne, and long-time Vatican official with the Pontifical Council for the Family, has worked selflessly to help produce "THE MASS: IN ALL ITS TREASURES."

An equally esteemed colleague of many years with CCSP is Dr. William E. May, McGivney "Professor" in the John Paul II Institute and a noted Moral Theologian who served for many years on the International Pontifical Institute and who is internationally renowned and respected in his field. Dr. May has contributed greatly to this publication and I am deeply grateful for his help, but especially for his friendship.

To my wife, Margaret, who, as in all our writings and publications, has applied her considerable knowledge of English, grammar and meaning, to this work. Tireless and selfless, it is as much her product as mine and her constant aid is always given with love and patience toward an "impatient fellow."

Finally, but with gratitude, we acknowledge the generous approval of the SACRED HEART MESSENGER in granting permission to draw on "...in whole or in part" their booklet "DAILY MASS." Now out of print, their booklet was published by the predecessor organization, "IRISH MESSENGER" and it has been of substantial benefit in the preparation of "THE MASS: ITS MYSTERIES REVEALED."

The many other persons who have aided in this work are remembered in our hearts and in our prayers.

ENDORSEMENT

The booklet by George P. Morse, entitled "THE MASS: ITS MYSTERIES REVEALED" is a very good and fine book written in a spirit of living faith and love, giving the essentials of the rich and concise teachings of our Holy Faith, including the doctrine of the Church; of the Councils and the Church Fathers; the writings of Saints and other great Christian authors; and the Catechism of the Catholic Church; on the Holy Sacrifice of the Eucharist in all its dimensions, in order to help Catholics to better understand and appreciate this infinite Treasure of inestimable value for the whole Church, the entire world, and for each and every member of the faithful in their daily lives on their way of grace to eternal beatitude.

Sincerely in Christ,

Christoph Cardinal Schönborn
Archbishop of Vienna

INTRODUCTION

These words of presentation are a warm invitation to read and meditate on this booklet written by George P. Morse on the actuality of reviving the faith in the Eucharist, in "THE MASS: ITS MYSTERIES REVEALED."

The author, throuugh the Apostolate, CATHOLICS COMMITTED TO SUPPORT THE POPE, which he founded, with his wife, Margaret Morse, has gifted the Church with the publication of an eleven volume series of books which constitute a "PRECIS OF OFFICIAL CATHOLIC TEACHING" on all the essential points of our faith. They make available to theologians, seminarians, clergy and lay people pronouncements of the Magisterium along the ages and into the present time.

The author's zeal for the purity of the faith has led him to reflect on the way faith is actually lived in our Christian Communities. And he could not but observe how religious practice has been endangered by the loss of faith in the Sacrament of the Eucharist – the loss of a clear knowledge of what the Sacrifice of the Mass, Communion and the Real Presence truly mean.

His thoughts reflect the experience and insight of one who has been a prominent civil servant and an active Catholic; they also reveal his love for all those Christ wants to save through the giving of His Flesh and Blood.

This booklet – THE MASS: ITS MYSTERIES REVEALED – is indeed a valid contribution to the New Evangelization in which the Holy Father exhorts us all to get involved.

Edouard Cardinal Gagnon, P.S.S.

PREFACE

Many millions of Catholics attend Holy Mass. A great number do not appear to know fully what really is taking place on the altar. And that is precisely the message of this book. This booklet is not about what we can see. It is not about liturgical signs and symbols. Rather, it is about what is taking place *within* those signs and actions; about what is really important, or, shall we say, Who really matters? It is Jesus Christ and the Supernatural reality and grace present in every Mass.

You may read this booklet to re-discover timeless truths you first learned as a child. Or, you may read this booklet and be surprised to discover, for the first time, not only the meaning of the Holy Eucharist, but the power, the energy and the attractive splendor of this great Sacrifice.

The reader will note that sacred authors have been cited spanning the entire 2000 year history of the Church. These holy men and women witness to the unchanging truths of the Mass throughout the ages – truths affirmed by the Magisterium of the Church.

Some readers will be surprised to find that the main emphasis of this booklet is *not* on receiving the Holy Eucharist, or Holy Communion; nor is it on the unity and the community among the people caused by the Blessed Sacrament, as important as these elements are to a complete understanding of the Eucharist. However, there is a reason for this and that is to bring before the reader the essential truths taught by the Catholic Church about the Sacrifice, Transubstantiation and the Real Presence because it is only after we grasp these truths that we realize fully why we should receive the Eucharist and how it unites us to God and to one another.

This booklet may therefore be seen as an antidote to an unduly horizontal understanding of the Mass that reduces the Eucharistic celebration to the level of a community meeting and over-emphasizes the meal dimension.

We are all too familiar with this watering down of the Mass with its disastrous spiritual, pastoral and moral results. Now is the time to look more deeply at the Mass and to discuss and contemplate its "Mysteries." Through the grace of God, may this little booklet be a valuable aid to all in this worthy endeavor.

George P. Morse

THE MASS: ITS MYSTERIES REVEALED

What is the Mass? Why is it of such excellence and beauty and why is it essential to our salvation?

Conversely — in spite of the overwhelming evidence of its efficacy for our salvation throughout the many centuries — why do we so often treat the Mass so casually, even at times irreverently? This in spite of the fact that our Catholic teaching tells us that it is not only a miraculous event of unparalleled importance, but essential to our very salvation?

Is it because we have lost the sense of sacredness? Is it because the modern world has taken from us our belief in the Real Presence? Or because we have fallen in love with the pleasures of the world against which Christ warned us? Do we no longer believe in the reality of Satan and his power as the prince of this world?

It requires not only the gift of God's grace, but also our own prayerful concentration to know and to believe that it is truly God — our Divine Savior — Who is present there on the altar waiting to be received by me. It is Jesus, Body and Blood, Soul and Divinity, Who is humbling Himself to come to me. Do I know and do I believe this to be true?

Put another way: Do I really accept as a part of my Catholic faith what the Church has always taught and will always teach, namely, that at the very moment I see the priest at the altar, at the most sacred part of the Mass, that he is truly acting in the person of Christ, *in persona Christi,* to bring about the actual Sacrifice of Calvary. That the actual Passion, Death and Resurrection of Christ is about to occur in my very presence? And that the bread will no longer be bread and the wine no longer wine, but truly the Body and Blood of my Savior and Redeemer?

If I do believe, then I must be overwhelmed with awe and wonder and adoration and gratitude at the magnitude of what I shall soon experience: Receiving Jesus!

Do I eagerly wait, in humble anticipation, the moment of Holy Communion when "my Lord and my God" will enter my body, bringing His saving grace?

If I do, then I am blessed beyond measure with the sense of the Gift of Faith that few experience. But, it is a blessing we can surely gain through the merits of Jesus Christ by frequently and reverently attending Mass and receiving our Lord in the state of grace and with an unswerving concentration on what the Church teaches about the majestic mystery of the Eucharistic Sacrifice.

On the other hand, do I attend Mass with my thoughts and mind elsewhere – on the events and cares of the day? Do I come to the Mass unbelieving, or partially believing, or in doubt? Doubt that this apparent wafer of bread is truly God Almighty? Have I been so influenced by the world and its distractions that I no longer permit, or direct, my mind to focus on what the Mass really is?

If so, I am allowing priceless graces to be lost to me and I am even imperiling my immortal soul.

Let us be realistic. It is difficult throughout the Mass — and every Mass we attend — to maintain a constant and unswerving focus on the teaching of the Church and Christ concerning the Mass. There are distractions and there are personal problems and there is the skillful temptation of the devil to deny to us the treasures Christ offers us by our reverent attendance and worthy reception of His Body and Blood.

But the rewards are beyond price and our obligation is clear: to merit the benefits, we must fulfill the conditions. And every Mass attended worthily increases our treasure of graces!

The Mass, with its Mysteries Revealed, is truly our greatest means for attaining Salvation.

IT IS CHRIST WHO IS THE PRIEST

Let us consider what is happening in the Mass.

It is Christ Himself Who is the principal and actual Priest. Usually, we know the priest who we see at the altar and so it may be difficult for us to realize that he is but the visible representative of Christ, acting in the very person of Christ, *in persona Christi*.

At the ordination of the priest, he becomes partaker in Christ's priesthood, receiving a certain, but limited, communication of Christ's power. It is therefore not, strictly speaking, the priest's own, but Christ's power that he receives and exercises. He is acting in the Person of Christ when he says at the consecration, not "This is His Body," but, rather, "This is My Body." Similarly, in the Sacrament of Penance, he is speaking in the Person of Christ when he says, "I absolve you."

As Pope John Paul II taught in his Letter for Holy Thursday, 1980, *Domenicae Cenae*, 8: "The priest offers the Holy Sacrifice *in persona Christi*. This means more than offering 'in the name of' or 'in the place of' Christ. *In persona* means a specific sacramental identification with Jesus Christ, the eternal High Priest, Who is the Author and principal Subject of this Sacrifice of His, the Sacrifice, in truth, in which nobody can take His place."

We offer Mass through and with the priest. Thus, the *Catechism of the Catholic Church*, n. 1369, cites the teaching of the Council of Trent: "Through the ministry of priests the spiritual sacrifice of the faithful is completed in union with the sacrifice of Christ, the only Mediator, which in the Eucharist is offered through the priests' hands in the name of the whole Church, in an unbloody and sacramental manner until the Lord Himself comes."

St. John Chrysostom tells us that "The priest is only a minister, for He Who sanctifies and transforms the Victim is Christ Himself, Who at the Last Supper changed the bread into His flesh. The same He continues to do still. Therefore, when you see the priest, at the altar, think not that it is he who offers the Sacrifice, but believe that it is the Hand of Christ, invisible to mortal sight."

St. Augustine re-enforces our understanding of this great mystery: "Christ is the One Who offers; He is also the Offering."

The Council of Trent taught that the Sacrifice of the Cross and the Sacrifice of the Mass are one and the same, the same now offering by the ministry of priests Who offered Himself on the Cross.

Likewise, Pope John Paul II teaches us that: "The Eucharist is above all a sacrifice. It is the sacrifice of the Redemption and also the sacrifice of the New Covenant, as we believe and as the Eastern Churches clearly profess: 'Today's sacrifice,' the Greek Church stated centuries ago, 'is like that offered once by the only begotten Incarnate Word; it is offered by Him (now as then), since it is one and the same sacrifice.'"

Similarly, the *Catechism of the Catholic Church*, n. 1366, teaches us that "The Eucharist is thus a sacrifice because it represents (makes present) the sacrifice of the Cross, because it is its memorial and because it applies its fruit."

When we speak of "memorial" with respect to the Mass, we do not mean a monument, or a plaque on a wall, or a mere human memory. We mean a re-presentation, or re-enactment, that really makes present what the Church recalls and celebrates; that is, the life, death and resurrection of Jesus Christ (cf. *Catechism of the Catholic Church*, n. 1356-1381). This is what He really meant when He said: "Do this in memory of Me" and ordained the Apostles as His first Priests.

This is what the Mass is. Therefore, when I participate worthily in the Mass, I am present, above all, at Calvary, with our Lady and Saint John, when they watched as Jesus Christ offered Himself for us. I am also present with the Apostles in the upper room when they welcomed the risen Lord. I am with them when He ascended into glory and when the Holy Spirit was poured out upon them. The work of our redemption and the source of our salvation are here made present, here in the Mass.

At the consecration of the bread and wine, it is Christ Himself Who is the priest offering Himself to the Father right before our eyes on the altar, through the priest.

It is Christ — actually present now — being crucified and rising from the dead in the miracle of the Resurrection and we are present, witnessing and sharing in this divine happening.

How can I comprehend and believe these awesome mysteries of which I am a part? Only because Christ has endured His suffering and is offering His one perfect Sacrifice for my salvation.

Clearly, I cannot comprehend all of this, but I must pray for the grace to believe and to accept the actuality of what is taking place and thus to participate worthily in this, the work of my salvation. In the Revelations of St. Mechtildis, our Lord, speaking of the Mass, is said to have addressed to her these consoling words:

> "I alone know and perfectly understand what this offering is that I daily make of Myself for the salvation of the faithful; it surpasses the comprehension of Cherubim and Seraphim and all the hosts of heaven."

Thus, we come to realize that by faith and belief in the words of Christ we come to know that when we receive the Holy Eucharist it is truly His Body and Blood that we are receiving.

In many parts of the world, the numbers of Catholics attending Mass and the numbers believing in the Real Presence have declined, but there will be no crisis in attendance at Mass — and no crisis in belief in the Real Presence — if we all strive to attend and participate in the Mass reverentially and worthily. And, if we do, will we not want to participate in the celebration of every Mass that we possibly can? Fulfillment of that commitment will bring the desire to influence those for whom we have an obligation to help come to know the priceless treasures which Christ has in store for each of us in the Holy Sacrifice of the Mass. What a marvelous way to respond to the plea of the Holy Father that we all join in the great command to Evangelize!

IT IS CHRIST WHO IS THE VICTIM

We know that it is Christ Who is the One who offers the Sacrifice. But, He is not only the Priest, He is also the Victim offered in the Mass as the oblation for our sins.

St. Augustine thus writes:

> "Who is the Priest, but that one Priest Who is both the Victim and the Priest."

And St. John Chrysostom says:

> "Christ was and is both Priest and Victim. He is the Priest according to the Spirit, the Victim according to the Flesh. He is both the Sacrificer and the Victim being sacrificed."

Pope John Paul II explains how Christ is Victim in the Eucharistic Sacrifice. "All who participate with faith in the Eucharist become aware that it is a 'sacrifice,' that is to say, a 'consecrated offering,' for the bread and wine presented at the altar and accompanied by the devotion and the spiritual sacrifices of the participants are finally consecrated so as to become truly, really and substantially, Christ's own Body that is given up and His Blood that is shed. Thus, by virtue of the consecration, the species of bread and wine represent in a sacramental unbloody manner the bloody propitiatory sacrifice offered by Him on the Cross to His Father for the salvation of the world. Indeed, He alone, giving Himself as a propitiatory victim, in an act of supreme surrender and immolation, has reconciled humanity with the Father, solely through His sacrifices, 'having cancelled the bond which stood against us.'" (Colossians 2:14, *Dominicae Cenae*, 9).

By the hands of the priest, Christ, the Victim, offers Himself to the Father. At the same time, *we* offer Christ, the Spotless Victim, to the

Eternal Father when we join in the sacrificial offering of each Mass.

Christ, Himself, the Man-God, is the Victim Who not only offers Himself, but all the merits of His life and Passion and Death, to His Eternal Father for our benefit.

Dear reader, if you will prepare yourself for the great mystery of the Mass by contemplating this beautiful act of humility by our all-powerful and loving God, taken in order to ensure our salvation, you cannot help but offer yourself, in turn, to your Savior and Redeemer. You will realize that, truly, the Mass is a sacrifice of infinite value.

In His love and humility, Christ pleads for us to seize every opportunity to join the Sacrifice of the Mass daily, whenever possible. He awaits our coming eagerly and with His boundless love.

THE SACRIFICE OF THE MASS IS IDENTICAL TO THE SACRIFICE OF THE CROSS

The Sacrifice of the Mass is not merely a commemoration of the Sacrifice of Calvary; it is identical with it, although differing from it in certain circumstances:

- It is identical in that:
  in both Sacrifices, the Priest is Jesus Christ, our Savior;
  in both Sacrifices, the Victim is the same, namely, Jesus Christ.

- It is different only in the manner of offering:
  on the Cross the Sacrifice of Christ consisted in the bloody offering of His life in an actual death, whereas, on the altar, it consists also in the offering of His Holy Humanity, but in an unbloody manner, to the mystical sacramental death represented by the two Eucharistic Species, His Body separated from His Blood;

  on Calvary, Christ offered Himself in His own natural and human form; on the altar, He offers Himself under the Veil of the Sacrament and by the ministry of visible priests;

  on Calvary, the Human Nature of Christ was susceptible of suffering and death; on the altar, His Human Nature is glorified and immortal; the Sacrifice of the Mass being consequently a Sacrifice free from physical pain.

The object of the Sacrifice of the Cross was to achieve the redemption of all people. This redeeming Sacrifice takes a sacramental form in the Mass because at the Last Supper this is the way Jesus Christ chose to apply to individuals all the grace He achieved, or merited, when He died once and for all for us.

The Mass is of infinite value because it is the same Sacrifice as Calvary. On the Cross, an inexhaustible fountain of eternal redemption was opened. In every age, from our eucharistic altars, this fountain perpetually pours forth its streams into the hearts of those who strive to take part worthily in the Sacrifice of the Mass.

Therefore, whatever Jesus Christ merited for us on the Cross is given to us abundantly in and through the Mass. We can claim this redeeming grace, not only for ourselves, but for those we love, both living and dead.

A key to this unity between the Cross and the Mass is the word "memorial" which we need to understand correctly.

The Catechism of the Catholic Church teaches that the Mass is a memorial in the deepest sense of a representation that makes present the saving events of Christ. (cf. n. 1366). Therefore, while in our terms of time and place, the Sacrifice of Calvary was offered in a land remote from us and at a time, some 2,000 years ago, the fact is that **every time we assist at Mass, anywhere, we are truly present at the Sacrifice of Calvary.**

The incomprehensible — to man — immensity of this mystery is deepened even more by the reality that the Sacrifice of Calvary — Passion, Death and Resurrection — is taking place now, before our eyes, in our presence. This is so because time and space do not exist in eternity where the great saving events of the past are forever present. This means we are truly there witnessing Christ's Passion, Death and Resurrection. In the Mass, we are raised into the dimension of eternity. And so, at the elevation, we respond in faith as we declare from our inmost heart: MY LORD AND MY GOD!

The Catholic Church has always taught that a valid Mass celebrated according to the Roman Rite, or a venerable Eastern Rite, is:

- not merely a memorial service for a past event;
- not a theatrical re-enactment of a past event;

- not a mystical death-burial-resurrection-ascension ceremonial;
- not merely a celebratory meal when we remember Christ;
- not a mere offering of bread and wine;
- not a mere memorial of the Last Supper.

On the contrary, when we take part in the Mass, we are actively participating in the saving death of Jesus, in His glorious Resurrection and Ascension. These events are not made present because of our faith. Rather, they are present because Jesus Christ, the Priest and Victim, is really present. Our faith enables us to perceive Him. It is faith that allows believers to perceive and understand and participate in the marvel of the Mass, but the presence of Christ in the Mass is not brought about by our faith.

Every day of every year, there are countless thousands of Masses celebrated making it possible for the participants to be present at the one and same event, namely, Christ's Death, Resurrection and Ascension. The same event that took place only once historically will never — can never — take place again. It cannot take place again — it need not take place again.

Therefore, dear Catholic believer, when the magnitude of this fact sinks home in your mind, you must forever wonder: How can I but kneel in awe before the sacrificial death of our Lord and Savior, Jesus Christ?

How can I lose any opportunity to assist at Holy Mass and to adore my Divine Savior while at the same time reaping the "boundless ocean of spiritual treasures" which await me in the Sacrifice of the Mass?

THE MYSTERIES OF THE MASS

The Holy Mass is without equal as the greatest marvel throughout all the world, in all history. The wonder of its mysteries is described in this way by St. Bonaventure:

> "The Holy Mass is as full of mysteries as the ocean is of drops, or as the sky is full of stars, or the courts of heaven are of angels. For in it so many mysteries are daily performed that I should be at a loss to say whether greater or more lofty wonders have ever been accomplished by Divine Omnipotence."

The great Jesuit theologian Sanchez says:

> "In Holy Mass, we receive treasures so wonderful and so real, gifts so divine and so costly, benefits so many appertaining to this temporal life, hope so certain for the life which is to come, that without faith it would be impossible for us to believe these assertions to be true. Just as one may take from the sea, or from a river all the water one needs, not only without exhausting it, but even without in the least diminishing its volume, so is it with the Holy Mass. So immeasurably great is it that it can suffer no diminution or exhaustion of its plenitude."

It is both important and instructive to examine these major Mysteries of the Mass:

First Mystery: In the Mass Christ Renews His Incarnation

The Second Vatican Council tells us: "For it is the liturgy through which, especially in the Divine Sacrifice of the Eucharist, 'the work of our redemption is accomplished'" (*Constitution on the Sacred*

Liturgy, 1).

What is this "Work of our Redemption?" It is not only the Passion and Death of our Lord, but it is His Incarnation, Birth and Life among us that is accomplished and renewed at every Mass.

St. Bonaventure tells us: "God appears to do no less a thing when He deigns daily to descend from heaven upon our altars than He did when He came down from heaven and took upon Himself our human nature."

According to St. John Damascene: "If I am asked how bread is changed into the Body of Christ, I answer: 'The Holy Ghost overshadows the priest and operates in the same manner in the elements which He effected in the womb of the Virgin Mary.'"

And what about me? Do I know — truly know and believe — what our Catholic faith teaches; namely, that, while before the consecration what the priest holds in his hands, and in the chalice, is only bread and wine, and that the moment he pronounces the sacred words of consecration bread and wine are no longer present, but in their place the living Body and Blood of the Man-God! Do I know and believe?

If I do not so believe, I must, in humble prayer, ask our Divine Savior for the grace to believe and continue praying until that certainty of belief comes to me — as it surely will.

And if I do believe, I must, in gratitude, thank God for the greatest of all treasures, namely, the belief in the Real Presence — the means of our salvation.

If I do believe, with joy I will fulfill the happy obligation of Mass every Sunday and seek the great opportunity for daily Mass as often as possible. I will participate in the liturgy fully, consciously and actively. Through worthy confession and devout prayer, I will prepare myself for the great gift of receiving our Lord Jesus Christ, knowing that He is truly present in the Blessed Eucharist.

Knowing that He is truly present in the tabernacle, or monstrance, my genuflection will be made with humble reverence before the King of kings, the Lord of lords, my Savior and my Judge. Knowing that He is truly present in the tabernacle, I shall make time and effort to visit and adore Him. Thus, by such prayer and adoration, I will be impelled to receive Him more frequently and reverently in the Sacrament of His Divine Love.

With the fuller realization of these great gifts given to me by Him, I will share the truth of His Real Presence not only with those for whom I have the obligation to teach the faith, especially my children and family, but with the friends I know who are yearning for the peace and joy and love of God. And I must be mindful of the teaching of Christ to "teach all peoples" and evangelize the world. And how better to do that than by sharing our knowledge of the Real Presence and the treasures of the Mass?

Then shall I surely see the Eucharistic fruits of mutual charity, unity and peace flourishing in our family, our parish, our community!

Second Mystery: In the Mass Christ Renews His Nativity

How often have we envied the privilege granted to the Shepherds and the Magi to visit at the crib of our Divine Savior and offer Him their adoration! We envy them also the graces and blessings they doubtless received. But, every day that we participate worthily at Mass, we, too, may receive a privilege equally as great as theirs; in fact, far greater because we may receive the actual Body and Blood of our Savior in the Sacrament of the Eucharist.

Pope St. Leo the Great said:

> "We do not seem to regard the birth of Christ as an

event of the past, but as one present to our sight. For we have proclaimed to us what the Angel announced to the shepherds: 'Behold, I bring to you tidings of great joy: this day is born to you a Saviour!' *Every day we may be present at this happy birth*, every day our eyes may behold it, if we will but go to Mass. *For then, it is in very deed renewed*, and by it the work of our salvation is carried on."

St. Jerome said: "The priest calls Christ into being by his consecrated lips." Pope Gregory XV confirmed this thought with the prayer he urges the priest to say before Mass: "I am about to celebrate Mass and to call into being the Body and Blood of our Lord Jesus Christ," which means to bring Christ into a place where He was not sacramentally present at the time. It is not surprising that the Church has us repeat the song of praise with which the Angels greeted the birth of the Savior in Bethlehem: "Glory to God in the highest, and peace to His people on earth."

Thus, when we worthily participate in the Mass, we can well imagine that we hear the Angel's words:

> "I bring you good news of ... great joy; for to you is born this day ... a Savior, Who is Christ the Lord ... you will find a babe wrapped in swaddling cloths and lying in a manger." (Luke 2, 10-2).

In the Holy Sacrifice of the Mass, we shall find the Infant wrapped in the swaddling clothes of the outward appearances of bread and wine; we shall find Him laid within the humble manger of the linen and sacred vessels on the altar; we shall find Him in the hands of the priest and, more marvelous and mysterious yet, we shall welcome Him as the Divine Food of His faithful people. What an overwhelming example of the perfect and total humility by the Almighty God Who is our Lord, our Savior and our Redeemer. What a priceless gift which is given to us asking in return only our total love!

Third Mystery: In the Mass Jesus Christ Renews His Life

In so many ways, the Mass is a reflection of the Life of Christ and the manner in which His life is renewed.

"Holy Mass," Bishop Fornerus said, "is a brief epitome of our Lord's Life, a recapitulation in one short hour of what He did during the thirty-three years He spent on earth."

Denis the Carthusian wrote in similar vein: "The whole life of Christ which He led upon earth was one long celebration of the Mass, He being Himself the Altar, the Priest, and the Victim."

Father Sanchez, writing on the same subject, says:

> "He who desires to profit by Holy Mass will be able to obtain forgiveness of sins and the gift of divine grace just as readily by assisting at it devoutly as if he had in person witnessed all the scenes of our Lord's life,"

The most dramatic and instructive lesson may be obtained from the beautiful liturgy of Saint John Chrysostom, celebrated by so many Byzantine Rite Catholics. Each step of the solemn celebration of the Mass according to this Rite is popularly seen as representing the life journey of our Lord and Savior.

The preparation of the priest and of the bread and wine at the table of prothesis before Mass, represents our Lord taking our flesh and assuming our mortality. In the Liturgy of the Word, we see His ministry of teaching and healing culminating in the revelation of the truth of His Gospel. The "little entrance," or Gospel procession, represents our Lord entering Jerusalem on Palm Sunday.

The Liturgy of the Eucharist begins with the "great entrance," or procession of the gifts of bread and wine, while the cherubic hymn is sung by the choir. This sacred action represents our Lord entering into His Paschal Mystery, as He goes up to Calvary to offer Himself, true Priest and Victim, to His Father. In the Eucharistic Prayer, the Sacrifice of Christ on the Cross, His glorious Resurrection and the outpouring of the Holy Spirit, are made present. Then, our great High Priest takes His people with Him into the glory of heaven as they become one with Him by receiving His Blessed Body and Blood in the Holy Eucharist.

How beautiful is this allegorical understanding of the Byzantine Liturgy. How clearly it shows us that every Mass, in whatever Catholic Rite it is celebrated, is a recapitulation, or renewal, of the life of Jesus Christ, our Savior.

Fourth Mystery: In the Mass Christ Intercedes For Us

"We have an Advocate with the Father, Jesus Christ, the Just, and He is the propitiation for our sins." (1 John 2, 1,2).

With these words, St. John provides us with a comforting assurance which we find literally and fully verified in the Mass.

Whenever the Sacrifice of the Mass is offered, so often does Christ plead for those who offer it and those for whom it is offered. That is, He pleads for the priest who offers it and for the people who assist at the Divine Sacrifice, and for those for whom it is offered by the priest.

Just reflect: Jesus Christ, our Savior and Redeemer, at every Mass we attend, pleading as our Intercessor with the Father for our well-being and salvation! If we believe the teaching of the Catholic Church, how can we fail to go to our knees everyday of our lives in grateful thanksgiving for our all-loving God? How we must strive to attend Mass at every opportunity! To do otherwise is to reject treasures beyond any this world can offer.

This is how St. Laurence Justinian describes our Lord's Eucharistic intercession:

> "When Christ is spiritually slain upon the altar, He calls upon His Heavenly Father; He shows Him His wounds that, by virtue of His earnest supplication, many may escape eternal damnation."

What an overwhelming gesture of generosity — a gift that is ours just for the taking. But how often we refuse. How often we attend Mass with neglect, indifference and boredom.

Christ was born, suffered and died for the salvation of the human race — to bring all souls to heaven. Constantly, He prayed to the Father. Often He spent the entire night in prayer and "in the daytime, He was teaching in the Temple" (Luke 21:37). On the Cross, He prayed when He suffered and died to save me from my sins and, at every Mass, He renews these prayers and supplications.

From our viewpoint, by assuming the humble appearances of bread and wine, He subjects Himself to profound humility in His Eucharistic presence on the altar. This, too, reflects what happened on the Cross: "I am become a worm and no man," He says through the lips of David, "the reproach of man and the outcast of the people" (Ps. 21:7).

According to one sacred author: "In this humble form, in this extreme abasement, Jesus speaks from the altar in a voice so powerful that it pierces the clouds, rends the heaven and opens to us the Divine mercy."

"Opens to us the Divine mercy" — for our salvation, a salvation that is ours for the asking if we but just assist at Mass worthily and often.

Fifth Mystery: In the Mass Christ Renews His Passion and Death

The Council of Trent clearly teaches:

> "Whosoever shall say that the Sacrifice of the Mass is only a remembrance of the Sacrifice of the Cross, let him be anathema.... In this Divine Sacrifice which is celebrated in the Mass, the same Christ is contained and immolated in an unbloody manner Who once offered Himself in a bloody manner on the Altar of the Cross.... The Victim is one and the same, the same now offering Himself by the ministry of priests Who offered Himself on the Cross, the manner alone of offering being different" (Session 22).

The Fathers of the Church are emphatic in their declaration of this truth as we see in the words of St. Gregory: "Although Christ dies not again, yet He suffers again for us in the Sacrifice of the Mass in a mysterious and mystical manner."

Theodoret adds this: "We offer no other Sacrifice than that which was offered on the Cross."

Let us repeat the words of St. Laurence Justinian: "When Christ is immolated on the altar, He speaks to His Father, He shows Him the marks of His wounds on His sacred Body, that by His intercession we may be saved from eternal torment."

Sixth Mystery: In the Mass Christ Renews the Shedding of His Precious Blood

In light of what has been said, we know that in the Mass is renewed the shedding of the Precious Blood. At the consecration of the Chalice, the priest repeats the very same words which Christ Himself used at the Last Supper: "This is the cup of my Blood, the Blood of the new and everlasting covenant which will be shed for you and for all so that sins may be forgiven."

The priest utters these words, not as merely quoting the words of our Divine Savior at the supper table, but as speaking and acting in His Person, and actually applying them to the sacrificial act in which he is engaged. Moreover, just as the first portion of the sentence, "This is the cup of My Blood," is absolutely true, and certainly and literally fulfilled, so, too, is it with the second part, namely, "Which will be shed for you and for all so that sins may be forgiven."

Consequently, it is true to say that, in the Mass, the Precious Blood of Christ is not only present, but is truly, though in a mystic manner, shed "for you and for all," that is to say for "you," the priest, and the congregation who are actually present at the Mass and for many others who are absent, especially those for whom the Mass may be offered even though they are not present.

What a powerful incentive and inducement for us to be present at the Holy Sacrifice as often as we possibly can and to participate worthily and devoutly. It is well to remember and meditate on the powerful words in the *Imitation of Christ* (Thomas a Kempis, Bk. iv., chap. 2):

> "As often as thou sayest or hearest Mass, it ought to seem to thee as great, as new, and as wondrous as if Christ, that same day, hanging on the Cross, was suffering and dying for the salvation of men."

St. Ambrose tells us: "As often as the Blood of Christ is shed, it is shed for the remission of sins."

Thus, the Precious Blood of Christ is shed for me in every Mass — and for the remission of my sins — and, to use the words of St. John Chrysostom, "Drawn for my cleansing from His sacred side."

How unspeakably sad we shall be on Judgment Day if we do not avail ourselves of every opportunity to assist devoutly and worthily at the Sacrifice of the Mass.

Seventh Mystery: In the Mass Christ Renews His Resurrection and Ascension

After the consecration, in each of the Eucharistic prayers, we find reference to the Resurrection of our Lord and Savior. In the Roman Canon, or First Eucharistic Prayer, and in the Third and Fourth Eucharistic Prayers, the Ascension is added to the Resurrection. Here, in the Liturgy, we find a deeper dimension of the Mysteries of the Mass.

The "Great Memorial" of the Eucharistic Offering includes not only making present the Passion and Death of our Lord, but His glorious Resurrection and Ascension into Heaven. The same Body nailed to the Cross rises glorious and immortal, the glorified human flesh of our Great High Priest who then shows Himself to His Apostles and then enters Heaven to intercede forever for us.

This should not be surprising when we reflect on what has already been noted, namely, that it is the risen Christ Who is really present on our altars under the appearances of bread and wine. When we read the Gospels, we see how the risen Christ was not confined by the limits of time and space and matter. He could and did appear wherever He wished and passed through material objects. This is the key to understanding how the same Christ can be present on many altars, in so many Masses, at the same time and in countless places all around the world.

This reality is beautifully expressed in the following stanzas from the hymn of St. Thomas, *"Lauda Sion, Salvatorem"*:

> Here beneath these signs are hidden
> Priceless things to sense forbidden;
> Signs, not things, are all we see:
> Blood is poured and flesh is broken,
> Yet in either wondrous token
> Christ entire we know to be.
>
> Whoso of this food partakes
> Does not rend the Lord, nor breaks;
> Christ is whole to all who taste:
> Thousands are, as one, receivers,
> One, as thousands of believers
> Eats of Him who cannot waste.
> . . . .
>
> When the sacrament is broken,
> Doubt not, but believe 'tis spoken,
> That each sever'd outward token
> doth the very whole contain.

The risen Christ is really present in both parts of the Host after it has been broken. Likewise, He is equally present under the appearances of both bread and wine. Therefore, consuming either the Host or the Precious Blood, we receive the whole Christ.

> Yet in either wondrous token
> Christ entire we know to be.

Unlike the Apostles gathered in the upper room, we do not see the Risen Lord. He is hidden from us under the humble appearance of food and drink. But, how we should rejoice, as the Apostles rejoiced in the upper room, whenever we meet the Risen Lord in the Mass. Like the Apostles at Emmaus, we can say, "Did not our hearts burn within us while He talked to us on the road, while He opened to us the Scriptures?" And, can we not joyfully proclaim, with them, how the Lord Jesus was known to us in the breaking of the bread? (cf. Luke 24: 32-35).

Yet more marvelous still, in the Holy Mysteries of the Mass, His broken Body and outpoured Blood offered up for us is offered also to us as the Sacrament of immortality. The Risen Christ is our food for eternal life. According to His solemn promise, "He who eats My flesh and drinks My blood has eternal life, and I will raise him up at the last day." (cf. John 6: 54).

When we worthily receive Christ in the Holy Eucharist, we are not only united in the best way with His saving death, but with His Resurrection. We are one with the Risen Lord, Who abides in us as we abide in Him. (cf. John 6:56).

Therefore, this final Mystery we have considered does not only look back to the past, but points us to the future. The Mass leads us on our pilgrimage through this life to the next in celebrating the great Paschal Mystery of Christ's Death, Resurrection and Ascension. We wait in joyful hope until He comes in glory. And, if we have faithfully participated in these Holy Mysteries while on earth, how great shall our hope be that our Merciful Judge will count us worthy to stand with Mary and the Saints in the glory of His Kingdom. It is not only the Eternal Priesthood of Christ that we celebrate in each Mass, but also His Universal Reign as our King.

THE FOUR PURPOSES FOR WHICH THE SACRIFICE OF THE MASS IS OFFERED

What are the purposes for which the Mass is offered?

1. To Give Honor and Glory to God.

2. To Thank Him for His Innumerable Benefits.

3. To Make Reparation for Our Many Sins.

4. To Seek Graces and Blessings Through Our Lord Jesus Christ.

Let us explore more fully each of these four purposes:

1. To Give Honor and Glory to God.

It is through the Mass, more than in any other way, that we fulfill this end. Fr. Sanchez tells us: "The homage that we pay to God, the glory that we give Him in the Mass, is so great that no greater service, no greater honor, could be shown Him upon earth."

St. Laurence Justinian states: "It is certain that nothing gives God greater glory than the spotless Victim of the altar, which Christ ordained to be sacrificed in order that His Church might offer praise to God."

The fact that we cannot offer higher praise to God than by celebrating, or assisting at, the Holy Sacrifice is made clear by Fr. Molina: "In the Mass, the first-born Son of God is offered to the Father with all the praise and glory which He rendered Him on earth." Obviously, this praise was infinite and in every way worthy of the Divine Majesty since it was offered by the Man-God. Therefore, "it follows that one Mass gives more honor and praise to God than all the efforts of all creatures to the end of time and through eternity."

While it is unquestionably true that the worship given to God by all the saints of heaven is inconceivable apart from Christ's Redemptive Sacrifice on Calvary, i.e., the Sacrifice of the Mass, nevertheless, in order to appreciate more fully the powerful significance of the Mass, it is beneficial to consider this dramatic explanation by a learned writer of the Seventeenth Century:

> "If all the powers of heaven should unite to form a solemn procession in honor of the Holy Trinity, at the head of which would be the Mother of God, the Chief of all creatures, surrounded by the Nine Choirs of Angels, followed by innumerable companies of the Saints and Blessed singing with the sweetest voices, playing on the most melodious instruments, this triumphant procession would doubtless be pleasing in His sight. But, if at the close of the procession, the Church Militant were to commission one single priest to say one Mass in honor of the Ever Blessed Trinity, this one priest, with his one Mass, would offer an incomparably higher tribute of praise than that glorious procession had done. Nay, it would be as far superior in glory and sublimity as the Son of God is exalted above all created things."

With this powerful statement, we are able to grasp at least slightly how transcendent is the praise and glory that we offer to God by just a single Mass, and how eager we should be to assist as often as possible at the Holy Sacrifice.

As the *Catechism of the Catholic Church* teaches: "The Eucharist is the sacrifice of praise by which the Church sings the glory of God in the name of all creation. This sacrifice of praise is possible only through Christ: He unites the faithful to His person, to His praise, and to His intercession, so that the sacrifice of praise to the Father is offered *through* Christ and, *with* Him, to be accepted *in* Him." (n. 1361).

2. To Thank Him for His Innumerable Benefits

How can we ever give adequate thanks to God for all He has given to us?

He created us in the dignity of being "little less than the angels" in heaven. He redeemed us from hell and the slavery of Satan at the cost of His terrible suffering and crucifixion and humiliation. He has given us the incomparable Gift of Faith along with innumerable means of securing our salvation: the Sacraments, especially the Blessed Eucharist and the Mass itself, and the boundless assistance of His own Mother and the Angels and the Saints, together with the Vicar of Christ and a Catholic Church guaranteed to stand against the very gates of Hell.

He gives us graces every day of our lives — graces to love Him, to avoid sin, to develop a right conscience and to know the way to love and serve Him. He gives us all of the physical benefits we need and responds to our pleas for health, protection and relief from worry for ourselves and our family. He has provided a world of beauty and bounty. But, above all, He has given us the Mass and the capacity to learn and know of its pre-eminence as the perfect means of showing to Him our gratitude.

"What shall I render to the Lord for all He has given to me?" asks the Psalmist. And He answers: "I shall take the cup of Salvation and invoke the name of the Lord" (Ps. 115: 3). Again: "Offer to God the sacrifice of praise, and pay thy vows to the Most High" (Ps. 49:14).

The true "cup of Salvation" is the Chalice of the Precious Blood, offered up by Christ to His Eternal Father in the Mass. The true "sacrifice of praise" is that which is daily offered on the altar.

"The Eucharist is a sacrifice of thanksgiving to the Father, a blessing by which the Church expresses Her gratitude to God for all His benefits, for all that He has accomplished through creation, redemption, and sanctification. Eucharist means, first of all, 'thanksgiving.'" (*Catechism of the Catholic Church,* n. 1360).

Surely, we must know how unspeakably great are God's benefits to us and how imperative is the duty we are under to thank Him to the very utmost of our power. To neglect this duty is not only wrong, but dangerous to our salvation.

Many great saints have warned us that, in consequence of our ingratitude, God withholds from us His graces and blessings, firstly, through just punishment and, secondly, in mercy, lest He should have to chastise us for our ingratitude. Many of our misfortunes are the result of our ingratitude while a grateful response to His kindness opens up the "fountains of His mercy."

This section on the Second Purpose can best be summarized by reading the eloquent and moving words of the great Jesuit writer, Fr. Segneri:

> "Consider Christian, how indebted we are to our Saviour for the institution of Holy Mass, for without it we can never thank God rightly for His benefits. It was the superabundance of His love that induced Him not only to load us with so many benefits, but to place within our reach the means of giving Him abundant thanks for these same benefits. Would that we appreciated our privileges and turned them to good account! When we hear Mass, Christ, Who is immolated to His Father for our sake, becomes our own, and with Him we become possessed of all His infinite merits, and are able to offer them to God the Father, thus to lighten the heavy load of our indebtedness that well nigh crushes us to earth."

3. To Make Reparation for Our Many Sins.

On this subject, the Council of Trent instructs us as follows:

> "The Holy Synod teaches that this sacrifice is truly propitiatory, and if one draws nigh unto God, contrite and penitent, He will be appeased by the offering thereof. He will be appeased by the offering thereof and, granting the grace and gift of penitence, will forgive even heinous crimes and sin." (Sess. 22, ch. 2).

Further on, in the same Session, the Council states:

> "If anyone says that the Sacrifice of the Mass is not a propitiatory sacrifice, let him be anathema." (Sess. 22, ch. 3).

In this regard, the same Council also teaches that, at the Last Supper, Christ instituted the visible Sacrifice of the Eucharist "by which the bloody Sacrifice which He was to accomplish once for all on the Cross would be re-presented, its memory perpetuated until the end of the world, and its salutary power be applied to the forgiveness of the sins we daily commit." (cf. *Catechism of the Catholic Church,* n. 1366).

Thus, while the Mass does not, in the case of mortal sin, supercede the necessity of going to confession, owing to the efficacious grace it gives, it may become the means of procuring perfect contrituion, which "obtains forgiveness of mortal sin if it includes the firm resolution to have recourse to sacramental confession as soon as possible." (*Catechism of the Catholic Church,* n. 1452).

At Mass, in the words and action of the liturgy, we see that this Holy Sacrifice is a true sacrifice of atonement for our sins. The celebration of Mass begins with a penitential rite in which we all confess our sins, and the celebrant responds, saying "May Almighty God have mercy on us, forgive us our sins and bring us to everlasting life." Again and again, we invoke the Divine Mercy, singing, or saying, "Lord have mercy!" in the Kyrie. Even in the Gloria, this same cry for pardon is woven into our praise of Jesus Christ, the slain Lamb of God (cf. Revelation 5: 6-10). This theme continues in other prayers throughout the holy liturgy, especially when we sing, or say, "Lamb of God, You take away the sins of the world: have mercy on us." And when, before Holy Communion, the priest shows us the Host and says, "This is the Lamb of God Who takes away the sins of the world." (cf. John 1:29).

St. Thomas Aquinas teaches: "The special effect of the Holy Sacrifice of the Mass is that it operates our reconciliation with God." Because there is one reconciling Sacrifice, the Cross, given to us in the sacramental form of the Mass, we hear words in the liturgy reminding us of the reconciliation between God and Man. In the Third Eucharistic Prayer, we ask the Father to "look with favor on Your Church's offering and see the Victim Who has reconciled us to Himself." And we beseech the Father saying: "May this sacrifice which has made our peace with you advance the peace and salvation of all the world . . . ." Thus, the Church teaches that the Mass is truly a reconciling, peace-making sacrifice, a true propitiation for our sins.

It is in the Mass, knowingly and devoutly attended, that we, as sinners, find our greatest aid to salvation.

"Knowingly" — that is, understanding the Mass and seeking to penetrate its great mysteries; "devoutly" — that is, attending with meditation, preferably before Mass, on the Four Great Ends for which it is offered and putting our minds and hearts into Christ's mind and heart as we assist worthily.

Under these conditions, i.e., when we assist "knowingly" and "devoutly", the Mass blots out venial sin.

This is especially true when we make a worthy Communion. Thus, the *Catechism of the Catholic Church,* n. 1394, teaches: "As bodily nourishment restores lost strength, so the Eucharist strengthens our charity, which tends to be weakened in daily life, and this living charity *wipes away venial sins.*"

Father Stratius says: "Such is the power of the Mass that our sins melt away before it as wax before the fire, and the penalties we have incurred are turned away from us." "Turned away from us" provided we take part in the Mass devoutly and receive the Holy Eucharist worthily, that is, fasting and with faith and contrition.

It is related in the life of the great mystic, St. Gertrude that, at the Elevation of the Sacred Host, she said: "Holy Lord God! I offer to Thee the Sacred Host for the remission of my sins," to which our Lord made known to her that, in answer to her prayers, her soul was cleansed from all stains and she was rendered worthy to be admitted to the embrace of her beloved Spouse.

With great merit, we may join the Angel who appeared to the three children at Fatima. As the Blessed Sacrament was suspended in the air before them, he prostrated himself and offered this beautiful prayer:

> "O most Holy Trinity, Father, Son and Holy Spirit, I adore you profoundly. I offer you the most precious Body, Blood, Soul and Divinity of Jesus Christ, present in all the tabernacles of the world, in reparation for the outrages, sacrileges and indifference by which He is offended. By the infinite merits of the Sacred Heart of Jesus and the Immaculate Heart of Mary, I beg the conversion of poor sinners."

4. To Seek Graces and Blessings Through Our Lord Jesus Christ.

This final Purpose for which the Mass is offered may be considered the "Treasures of the Mass", which we now explore.

Father Anthony Molina, in his work on the dignity of the priesthood, states:

> "There is nothing so profitable to mankind, so efficacious for the relief of the suffering souls, nothing so helpful for the attaining of spiritual riches, as the Most Holy Sacrifice of the Mass."

And, the Council of Trent:

> "No other work can be performed by the faithful so holy and divine as this great mystery itself, wherein that life-giving Victim, by which we were reconciled to the Father, is daily immolated on the altar by priests." (Sess. 22).

Cardinal Ratzinger, in his beautiful expression, says:

> "We know that the souls of those who have died are alive in the resurrected body of the Lord.
>
> The Lord's body shelters them and carries them toward the common resurrection.
>
> In this body which we are permitted to receive, we remain close to one another, and we touch each other."

The whole Church is united with the offering and intercession of Christ for all mankind (cf. *Catechism of the Catholic Church*, 1083, 1368, 1369). As we have already seen, He is our great High Priest Who intercedes for us. In the Mass, the greatest of all prayers, our prayers are joined to His perfect intercession on our behalf.

Let us now consider the effects of the intercessory purpose of the Mass:

a. Increases and Intensifies Our Life of Grace:

As the *Catechism of the Catholic Church* teaches, Grace may be understood as working principally in two ways: Sanctifying Grace and Actual Grace. (n. 2000).

> - Sanctifying Grace is the in-dwelling gift of the Holy Spirit and may be termed the spiritual life and treasure of the soul whereby we become the friends and children of God and the heirs to His Eternal Kingdom. In proportion to the degree of Sanctifying Grace present in the soul at the hour of death will be the greatness of its reward in heaven.
>
> Nothing can deprive us of this treasure except mortal sin. Every act of ours, performed with the help of God's grace and in the state of grace and with the proper disposition, adds something to this spiritual treasure in the soul. How much it adds depends largely on the nature of the act and the disposition with which it is performed. This grace invests the soul with a surpassing loveliness, makes it wonderfully dear to God, secures for it His strength and guidance and protection, ennobles it beyond conception, makes us, in a word, the "sons of God." (Rom. 8:17).
>
> - Actual Grace is an intervention by God giving to the will the spiritual impulse and illumination that enables us to do good works. "One single grace," says Saint Thomas, "is a greater good than all the other good

things of the world." The smallest grace is of infinitely greater value than all the silver, gold and jewels in existence.

The Fathers of the Church, as well as many spiritual writers, across the centuries up to the present time, have expressly affirmed that graces, Sanctifying and Actual, are received at Mass.

St. Cyril: "Spiritual gifts are freely given to those who assist at Mass reverently."

Pope Innocent III: "Through the power of the Holy Sacrifice of the Mass . . . we obtain a plenteous share of the fruits of grace."

In order to experience the "Fullness of the Mass," we must prepare ourselves for the effects of the treasures of grace which will accrue to us in the celebration of this Holy Mystery.

As the *Catechism of the Catholic Church* states: "The grace of the Holy Spirit seeks to awaken faith, conversion of heart, and adherence to the Father's Will. These dispositions are the pre-condition both for the reception of other graces conferred in the celebration itself and the fruits of new life which the celebration is intended to produce afterward." (n. 1098).

b. Increases Our Glory in Heaven:

This "treasure" is a result of our growth in our life of Grace. The Council of Trent confirms that "all the good works of one that is justified merit increase of grace and glory" (Sess. 6, ch. 24) and this is pre-eminently true of the greatest of "good works," by our participation in the Mass. Consequently, we add to our future glory and eternal happiness through every Mass we hear reverently and with proper disposition.

c. Secures for Us All the Graces and Blessings Necessary in Our lives:

In his characteristic classical language, Fr. Nicholas Gihr tells us:

> "The Holy Mass has always and everywhere been regarded as the most efficacious means to obtain assistance in all the necessities and concerns of life . . . . The Mass draws down upon the soul the light and the dew of heaven, so that all the gifts of the Holy Ghost therein attain their most beautiful bloom and ripeness. The Mass obtains grace, strength and courage to perform good works, to overcome the flesh and its concupiscence, to despise the world with its allurements and threats, to resist the attacks of Satan, to endure not only patiently, but with joy and thanksgiving to God, the hardships and troubles, the sufferings and evils, of this life; to fight the good fight, to finish our course, and to persevere in the way of salvation unto the end, and thus to bear off the crown of life and of eternal glory . . . . Thus, the Holy Sacrifice of the Mass is the most profound and significant expression of all our petitions and intercessions in spiritual and temporal concerns."

d. Gives Us the Assurance of a Happy Death:

The greatest and most comprehensive of all graces is to die a happy death in God's grace.

This ensures sublime happiness for all eternity!

Over the centuries, at the hour of death, the Catholic could have no greater consolation than the thought of the many Masses attended by the individual during his, or her, lifetime — Masses heard with devotion and with reverence. Today, many Catholics, sadly, live — and die — without the consolation, or even the realization, of this priceless "Treasure."

In fact, how many reflect on this precious truth and plan for a happy death?

The words of Pope St. Gregory, the Great regarding the Mass, can be of great comfort to those dying in the state of grace:

> "The Mass is uniquely powerful to procure for us all the graces and helps we need at the hour of our death. It applies to our souls the merits of Christ's own Blessed Passion and Death. It rescues the departing soul from the powers of evil, cleanses it from sin, obtains for it mercy and gives it a portion in life eternal."

Can we even begin to grasp the magnitude of the effects of the Mass in light of this statement?

The most effective preparation we can make for a happy death is to assist at Mass as often as we possibly can and to always receive the Holy Eucharist devoutly and worthily.

e. Is the Most Powerful Help of the Faithful Departed.

Purgatory. How seldom we hear about Purgatory. How seldom do we think about Purgatory and ponder its effects upon our eternal life.

How infrequently we pray for the poor souls in Purgatory — even for members of our own family and for our benefactors! The Church has long put a very high priority on prayers for the souls in Purgatory, especially on Mass and Communion because it is only through our prayers and sacrifices that our loved ones and all souls in Purgatory may have their sufferings ameliorated and be hastened to eternal glory with God.

It remains for us to make this beautiful practice a part of our daily life. The Council of Trent speaks of the Mass as the great means of helping the souls in Purgatory. "This Ecumenical Synod," it said, "teaches that the souls detained in Purgatory are helped by the suffrages of the faithful, but principally by the acceptable Sacrifice of the Altar."

Citing the same Council, the *Catechism of the Catholic Church* states the following:

> "The Eucharistic Sacrifice is also offered for the faithful departed who 'have died in Christ but are not yet wholly purified,' so that they may be able to enter into the light and peace of Christ." (n. 1371).

The *Catechism of the Catholic Church* further reminds us:

> "From the beginning, the Church has remembered the memory of the dead and offered prayers in suffrage for them; above all, the Eucharistic Sacrifice, so that, thus purified, they may attain the beatific vision of God. The Church also commends alms giving, indulgences, and works of penance undertaken on behalf of the dead ...." (n. 1032).

The Church has, down through the centuries, urged the faithful to pray and offer Masses for the souls in Purgatory — the "Church Suffering."

And so, it is within our power, and it is our obligation as an aid to our salvation, to bring aid and relief to the souls in Purgatory. And the most efficacious means to that end is through the Mass.

St. Cyril of Jerusalem gives the assurance that we pray "for all who have fallen asleep before us in the belief that it is a great benefit to the souls on whose behalf the supplications are offered, while the Holy and Tremendous Victim is present . . . ."

St. Thomas adds: "By no other oblation can the souls in Purgatory be more speedily relieved than by the Sacrifice of the Mass."

It should be for us a cause of joy and comfort to know that, by attending Mass frequently and with devotion, we may, more than by any other means, assist the suffering souls — either for all souls, or by specific names — and help bring them to a speedier enjoyment of the eternal bliss of Heaven.

We do not know what awaits each one of us in Purgatory. But, there, the blessed dead suffer in the refining fire of God's Love which is His eternal Mercy. They are passive, unable to help themselves. No longer can they merit for their own benefit. They yearn for the Beatific Vision and amidst their sufferings they know that Heaven will be theirs in time. But they must wait and be purified, a condition they welcome with joy because they know they can only come into God's presence when they have been freed of every mar and blemish and are in a totally purified state.

We must never forget that these souls are one with us in the Mystical Body of Christ. As members of Christ's Body, they can still benefit from His saving work on the Cross.

How is this possible? Through the Masses that are being offered every moment of every day throughout this world of time and space.

The Mass penetrates eternity. It is the greatest prayer for the holy souls because it applies the infinite power and value of the atoning

Sacrifice of the Cross to them. That is why the Church invites — urges — us to have Masses offered for the holy souls. Never let us forget that we have this way of really helping those we love and see no longer, those who are still one with us in "the Communion of Saints."

THE SACRIFICE OF THE WHOLE CHURCH

Dear reader, in light of these truths, we realize a greater appreciation of the "Fullness of the Mass," that incomparable Mystery of Christ's Love whereby all possible souls are brought to Eternal Life with Him.

The scope of Christ's Love helps us to realize that the Mass is the Sacrifice of the Church — the whole Church (cf. *Catechism of the Catholic Church* (nn. 1368-1369). And this leads us to the awareness that constantly millions of Catholics all around the globe, "from the rising of the sun until its setting" (Malachi 1:11), are offering the pure oblation to the Father, the Sacrifice of Jesus, His beloved Son. At every moment of every day, somewhere in the world, the Sacrifice of our Redemption is being renewed on an altar.

The whole Body of Christ offers this Sacrifice with, and through its Head, Jesus Christ. Moreover, in each particular Church on earth, gathered around the diocesan Bishop, the Mass is the Sacrifice of Unity, as you and I are a part of that Unity. The Second Vatican Council states: "In each altar community, under the sacred ministry of the bishop, a manifest symbol is to be seen of that charity and 'unity of the mystical body, without which there can be no salvation.'" (Dogmatic Constitution on the Church, *Lumen Gentium,* 26). To be "in communion" with the Pope and the bishops is to be able to share in the Sacrifice they offer and to receive the Body and Blood of Christ in the Sacrament of the Eucharist.

We must not, however, restrict this to the "Pilgrim Church" that we can see on earth. The Mass involves the "Church Triumphant" in Heaven, as well. In the Creed, we profess our belief in the communion of Saints. The Mass is the high point of our communion with the blessed dead. Therefore, the Eucharistic Prayer, or Canon, refers to Our Lady and the saints and angels who join us at every offering of the Sacrifice of the whole Church.

"In the Eucharist, the Church is, as it were, at the foot of the Cross with Mary, united with the offering and intercession of Christ." (*Catechism of the Catholic Church*, n. 1370).

Moreover, because the Lord's Sacrifice is offered for the dead, for the members of the "Church Expectant" being purified in Purgatory, our dear departed often seem so very close to us at the altar of God. Indeed, at no other moment in this passing life are they as close to us as when we are all one in the Sacrifice of the Mystical Body of Christ.

Remember, therefore, that every Mass is a Public Offering. In his Encyclical Letter on the Eucharist, *Mysterium Fidei*, 32, Pope Paul VI teaches:

> "For any Mass, even if celebrated by a priest in private, is not private; it is the act of Christ and the Church. The Church, indeed, in the Sacrifice which she offers, is learning to offer Herself as a universal sacrifice; she is also applying to the whole world, for its salvation, the redemptive virtue of the Sacrifice of the Cross, which is unique and infinite."

Because the Mass is the Sacrifice of the whole Church, it is thus aptly termed "our Sacrifice."

The Gift of Myself

We have considered the awesome wonders – yes, the "mysteries" – of the Mass and we now come to a final and inspiring truth:

It has been made possible for me to be able to offer myself to God in the Holy Mass!

Over and over, I ask myself the question: "How can this be?" How can I, a sinner, have the power to offer myself and by what means can

I do this?"

First, by my Baptism, I share, in a certain way, as a lay person, in the Priesthood of Jesus Christ. It is through the indelible character of my Baptism that I always have the right, the duty and the power to participate in the Mass. No sin of mine can take away the permanent character of Baptism which permits me to share in Christ's offering of Himself through the ministry of His ordained priest who, by virtue of Holy orders, is able to act in *personna Christi*. My life, my intentions, my hopes and fears, my joys and sorrows — these small offerings are taken into His Offering, the work of the Head of the Mystical Body, of which I am a living cell!

Second, in Baptism, I not only become a member of Christ's Body, the Church, but I was freed from Original Sin and inwardly transformed. Jesus, the Just One, inwardly justifies me, a poor sinner. Jesus, the Holy One, sanctifies me with His Holy Spirit. He, the Lamb Who alone is worthy, makes me worthy to offer, with and through the priest, who raises the Host and Chalice as he says, "Through Him, with Him, and in Him. . . ."

As a baptized Christian, I thus confidently enter the Lord's Sacrifice. As the author of the Letter to the Hebrews says:

> "Therefore, brethren, since we have confidence to enter the sanctuary by the Blood of Jesus, by the new and living way which He opened for us through the curtain, that is, through His flesh, and since we have a great Priest over the House of God, let us draw near with a true heart in full assurance of faith, with our hearts sprinkled clean from an evil conscience and our bodies washed with pure water." (Hebrews 10:19-22).

Thus, I join myself to His perfect offering simply by the act of faith involved in going to Mass and in taking part in the Eucharistic celebration.

The gift of my life is often described as symbolized in the gifts of bread and wine that are brought to the altar to be offered in order to be transformed into the Body and Blood of Christ. But we can go beyond this symbolism. With and through the distinct action of the ordained priest, I can make a priestly offering of my whole life to God. And so, at every Mass, the priest invites us to pray, as one approved English translation puts it: "that my sacrifice and yours may be acceptable to God the Almighty Father."

In the Eucharistic Prayer, we thus pray that the Father will "make us an everlasting gift" to Him. We do not offer ourselves by our own unaided efforts, but, empowered by the Father Who gives us the Holy Spirit through Jesus, His Son, we can make our lives a fragrant offering to God.

Of course the quality of my self-offering depends upon my response to God's gift of grace. By contrition and faith, by being at peace with my brothers and sisters, my offering is rendered acceptable in and through Christ's Perfect Offering. This is why the most complete way to make this self-offering is by receiving the Sacrament of the Blessed Eucharist. As Jesus Christ taught us: "He who eats my Flesh and drinks my Blood abides in Me and I in him." (John 6:56).

When we eat ordinary food, we transform it into ourselves. But, when we eat the Living Body of Jeses, He makes our mortal flesh come alive with His glorious life precisely because " 'the partaking of the Body and Blood of Christ does nothing other than transform us into that which we consume.' " (Vatican Council II, *Lumen Gentium*, n. 26, quoting Pope St. Leo the Great). We are thus one with the One Who offers!

When we become one with Christ through receiving His Body and Blood, the Holy Spirit makes us one with God and with one another.

"In the unity of the Holy Spirit," we offer the Lord's Sacrifice together with the priest so as to become the working Body of Christ in the world. And, so let us conclude with a final encouraging reflection that sums up the grace of the Sacrament of the Blessed Eucharist:

> At the moment of Communion, I not only receive Jesus Christ, but He receives me, insofar as He welcomes me to Himself and, in Eucharistic Union with Him, I give myself to God the Father. His one perfect Sacrifice absorbs and purifies my imperfect offering. Once we grasp this truth, every Mass can truly become a foretaste of the eternal worship of Heaven!

* * *

Dear reader,

Down through the many centuries since Christ first offered His precious Body and Blood to His disciples at the Last Supper, theologians, doctors of the Church, and religious and lay people have sought to explain the mysteries and the treasures of the Mass, in "All Its Fullness."

Their writings and teachings have contributed greatly to the love, the reverence, the understanding and the fidelity to the Mass by the faithful.

This booklet seeks not to approach the great contributions made by those learned teachers; rather, to provide an easy to read – and read often – statement, in the words of Cardinal Schönborn, in his ENDORSEMENT, "... giving the essentials of the rich and concise teachings of our Holy Faith ... on the Holy Sacrifice of the Eucharist in all its dimensions, in order to help Catholics to better understand and appreciate this infinite Treasure of inestimable value ... on their way of grace to eternal beatitude."

His Eminence, Cardinal Gagnon, in his INTRODUCTION, calls our attention to the tragic "... loss of faith in the Sacrament of the Eucharist – the loss of a clear knowledge of what the Sacrifice of the Mass, Communion and the Real Presence truly mean." His clear and stark statement provides the purpose for this small booklet which is written so that it can be read by Catholics, young and old, of great or modest learning, who have been born into faith, or come to its treasures lately, and so that it may be read often and in preparation for our participation in the great Mystery of the Mass.

As a further aid in preparing to receive our Sovereign Lord, our Savior and Redeemer, on the following pages we offer you prayers to say both before and after Communion. These prayers have long served to inspire Catholics to worthily and devoutly receive Jesus and to express our gratitude to Him for coming to us in Holy Communion.

PRAYERS BEFORE MASS AND HOLY COMMUNION

Prayer of St. Ambrose

0 gracious Lord Jesus Christ, I, a sinner, nothing presuming on my own merits, but trusting in Your mercy and goodness, with awe and trembling approach the table of Your most sweet feast. For my heart and body are stained with many sins; my thoughts and lips not diligently guarded. Wherefore, 0 gracious God, 0 awesome Majesty, in my extremity I turn to You the fount of mercy; to You I hasten to be healed and take refuge under Your protection; and You, before Whom as my Judge I cannot stand, I long for as my Savior.

To You, Lord, I show my wounds, to You I lay bare my shame. I know my sins are many and great, for which I am afraid. My trust is in Your mercies, of which there is no end. Look therefore upon me with the eyes of Your mercy, Lord Jesus Christ, God and man, crucified for man; hearken unto me whose trust is in You; have mercy upon me who am full of sin and misery, O fount of mercy, that will never cease to flow.

Hail, Saving Victim, offered for me and all mankind on the Cross of suffering and shame. Hail, noble and precious Blood, flowing from the wounds of my crucified Lord and Savior, Jesus Christ, and washing away the sins of the whole world. Be mindful, 0 Lord, of Your creature whom You have redeemed with Your own Blood.

I repent that I have sinned; I desire to amend what I have done. Take therefore away from me, 0 most merciful Father, all my iniquities and sins: that, being cleansed both in body and soul, I may worthily taste the Holy of holies; and grant that this holy feeding on Your Body and Blood, of which, unworthy as I am, I purpose to partake, may be for the remission of my sins and the perfect cleansing of all my offenses, for the driving away of all evil thoughts and the renewal of all holy desires, for the healthful bringing forth of fruit well-pleasing unto You, and the most sure protection of my soul and body against the wiles of all my enemies. Amen.

Prayer of St. Thomas Aquinas

O Almighty and Eternal God, behold I approach the Sacrament of Your only begotten Son, our Lord Jesus Christ. I come as one sick to the physician of life, as one unclean to the source of all mercy, as one blind to the light of the eternal sun, as one poor and needy to the Lord of heaven and earth.

I beseech You, therefore, out of the abundance of Your immense goodness, deign to heal my infirmity, cleanse me from my sins, illumine my blindness, enrich my poverty, clothe my nakedness. Grant that I may receive the Bread of angels, the King of kings, the Lord of lords, with as much reverence and humility, contrition and devotion, purity and faith, with such uprightness of purpose and intention, as may be profitable to the salvation of my soul.

Grant me, I beseech You, to receive not only the Sacrament of the Lord's body and blood, but also the grace and virtue of the Sacrament.

O most merciful God, grant me so to receive the body of Your only son, our Lord Jesus Christ, which He took from Mary, ever virgin, that I may merit to be incorporated into His mystical body, and numbered amongst His members.

O most loving Father, grant that Your beloved Son, whom, now hidden beneath the sacramental veil, I propose to receive, I may at length contemplate forever, face to face; Who with Thee lives and reigns in the unity of the Holy Spirit, God, world without end. Amen.

My Own Personal Prayer before Mass

Dear Father, as I prepare to participate in the Mass this day, please help me to know and concentrate on the reality of Your Divine Son's Passion, Death and Resurrection as He carries out Your Will in offering Himself to You in supplication for our salvation; as He, through the actions of the priest, becomes the oblation for our sins; and as the bread and wine become the Body and Blood of our Savior and Redeemer, as Calvary occurs now, in our presence, on this Altar.

Dear Father, help me to exclude all else from my mind and heart and to know that soon I shall receive Your Divine Son as He humbles Himself to come to me, Body Blood, Soul and Divinity, for my salvation.

Lord have mercy. Christ have mercy, Lord have mercy. Amen.

PRAYERS AFTER MASS AND HOLY COMMUNION

Prayer Before a Crucifix

Look down upon me, good and gentle Jesus, while before Your face I humbly kneel, and with burning soul pray and beseech You to fix deep in my heart live sentiments of faith, hope and charity, true contrition for my sins, and a firm purpose of amendment. Meanwhile, I contemplate with great love and tender mercy Your five most precious wounds, pondering over them within me, and calling to mind the words which David in prophecy made You say concerning Yourself, my Jesus: "They have pierced My hands and feet, they have numbered all My bones."

(Plenary Indulgence is granted for each Friday of Lent and Passiontide to the faithful who, after Communion, piously recite this prayer before an image of Christ crucified. On other days of the year, the indulgence is partial).

Anima Christi

Soul of Christ, be my sanctification;
Body of Christ, be my salvation;
Blood of Christ, fill all my veins;
Water from Christ's side, wash out my stains;
Passion of Christ, my comfort be,
O good Jesus, listen to me.
In Thy wounds, I fain would hide,
Ne'er to be parted from Thy side.
Guard me when the foe assails me;
Guide me when my feet shall fail me;
Bid me come to Thee above.
With Thy saints to sing Thy love, forever and ever.
Amen.
(Partial indulgence)

Offering of Holy Communion as Viaticum

My God! If I am to die today, or suddenly at any time, I wish to receive this Communion as my Viaticum. I desire that my last food may be the Body and Blood of my Savior and Redeemer; my last words, Jesus, Mary and Joseph; my last affection, an act of pure love of God and of perfect contrition for my sins, my last consolation, to die in Thy holy grace and in Thy holy love. Amen.

Prayer of St. Thomas Aquinas

I render thanks to You, O Lord, Holy Father, everlasting God, Who has vouchsafed, not for any merits of mine, but of Your great mercy only, to feed me, a sinner, Your unworthy servant, with the precious Body and Blood of Your Son, our Lord Jesus Christ; and I pray that this Holy Communion may not be for my judgment and condemnation, but for my pardon and salvation. Let it be unto me an armor of faith and a shield of good purpose, a riddance of all vices, and a rooting out of all evil desires; an increase of love and patience, of humility and obedience, and of all virtues; a firm defense against the wiles of all my enemies, visible and invisible; a perfect quieting of all my impulses, fleshly and spiritual; a cleaving unto You, the one true God; and a blessed consummation of my end when You call. And I pray that You will vouchsafe to bring me, a sinner, to that feast, where You, with Your Son and the Holy Spirit, are to Your holy ones true light, fullness of blessedness, everlasting joy, and perfect happiness. Through the same Christ our Lord. Amen.

O LORD I AM NOT WORTHY

Traditional
(arr. Don Capisco)

O Lord I am not worthy
That Thou shouldst come to me,
But speak the words of comfort
My spirit healed shall be.

And humbly I'll receive Thee,
The Bridgegroom of my soul,
No more my sin to grieve Thee,
Or Fly Thy sweet control.

O Sacrament most holy!
O Sacrament divine!
All praise and all thanksgiving
Be every moment Thine.